MW01470708

THE WILL OF
MAN

THE WILL OF
MAN

JOHNNY RUTLEDGE

authorHOUSE®

AuthorHouse™
1663 Liberty Drive
Bloomington, IN 47403
www.authorhouse.com
Phone: 1-800-839-8640

Published by AuthorHouse   08/21/2012

ISBN: 978-1-4772-6342-6 (sc)
ISBN: 978-1-4772-6344-0 (hc)
ISBN: 978-1-4772-6343-3 (e)

Library of Congress Control Number: 2012915551

Dedication

I would like to thank God for this book and all that it will do for those who will be blessed by it. I dedicate this book to my entire family especially my wife and children, not to mention the most precious people in the world to me, my grand children. All of them are exactly the reason why I wrote this book and I hope they will grow to be God-fearing adults. This book will be a guideline or a tool for them to use to make their lives easier. My prayers are that with this book, my grandson (JONOVAN RANDY RUTLEDGE) will not be defeated by his own will, but will become more than conquered because of what I have left him to understand, who and what he is in the LORD JESUS CHRIST, HIS LORD AND SAVIOR, and avoid the mistakes I made due to my lack of knowledge. To my oldest granddaughter, even when I am no longer here to teach you about life, my hope is that you will be a leader for your sister and cousins. This is why I dedicate my life and work to y'all, to preserve the integrity, the holiness, and the blessing of truth. Therefore, it is my greatest wish that each one of you will prosper, have good health and live a long and beautiful life.

Yours truly,
JOHNNIE LOULLIE RUTLEDGE (52 yrs. old)

(DRANDMADD!!!!!!!!!)
I LOVE Y'ALL . . .

 *When the will of man runs into the will of God, it is exposed and soon explodes.*

I have often wondered what in the world is this thing in me that controls me, that causes me to be just the opposite of what I always wanted to be. Could it be the will of man—my own will?

The will of man is like an iron bridge built with plastic rivets. When a person does not know his own will, it will lead to and cause his destruction. The human will was made to destroy its host. Man, know thyself and live . . .

What is this will, and where exactly is it? These questions, more than any others, stand out in my mind, and I am totally committed to the quest of finding answers to them. First and foremost, I wish to explore the possibility that the human will is actually a distinct, spiritual, functioning organ that hides itself within a man's heart or mind. It's very name, "will," means that it will be hindered by its own design, as revealed in the words of Jesus in Matthew 26: 36–39: The New King James Version—JR

Jesus came with them to place called Gethsemane and said to the disciples, "Sit here while I go and pray over there," and took with him two sons of Zebedee, and he began to be sorrowful and deeply distressed. Then he said to them, "My soul is exceedingly sorrowful, even to death. Stay here and watch with me." He went a little farther and fell on his face and prayed, saying, "O my father, if it is possible, let this cup pass from me; nevertheless not as I will, but as you will."

[36] Then Jesus came with them to a place called Gethsemane, and said to the disciples, "Sit here while I go and pray over there." [37] And He took with Him Peter and the two sons of Zebedee, and He began to be sorrowful and deeply distressed. [38] Then He said to them, "My soul is exceedingly sorrowful, even to death. Stay here and watch with Me."

[39] He went a little farther and fell on His face, and prayed, saying, "O My Father, if it is possible, let this cup pass from Me; nevertheless, not as I will, but as You *will*."

We are all thankful that Jesus rejected his own will and allowed his father's will to be—that God's will ruled over human will. The will of man was engineered to be destroyed; by its own design, it will be destroyed. When man came with his will to the earth, he was like fruit fallen to the ground and left there; without any assistance, that fruit is sure to die and never reproduce. And it speaks volumes about the one that sent man—or, should I say, created him. Just like the seed that God creates, which is deposited beneath the soil so the fruit can live again, man is sure to die if God does not assist in his development. Without God there would not be man, and without God man cannot sustain himself.

Maybe man would be more like God if he could master his own will and command it to remain constant all the time. But it seems to me that this is one of the problems man encounters when he is faced with a decision: as soon as the opportunity presents itself, he almost always chooses according to his own will, not God's. So I often wonder if we were given this will to go astray. Maybe God wants us to see what it is like to do the opposite of what he wants us to do. I'll admit that while I don't know what God was after, I seem always to know what I am after—or, as the Apostle Paul says in Romans 7:18–20, "For I know that in me [that is, in my flesh] nothing good dwells; for two wills are present with me. How to perform what is good I do not find. For the good that I will to do, I do not do: but the evil I will not to do I practice. Now if I do what I will not to do; it is no longer I who do it, but the sin that dwells in me." [18] For I know that in me (that is, in my flesh) nothing good dwells; for to will is present with me, but *how* to perform what is good I do not find. [19] For the good that I will *to do,* I do not do; but the evil I will not *to do,* that I practice. [20] Now if I do what I will not *to do,* it is no longer I who do it, but sin that dwells in me. In verses 21 through 24, Paul goes on to surrender to the very thing that causes him the most pain—his own will. We watch Paul struggle with this inward man, which he calls "sin" or "flesh," and finally he declares that with the mind he serves the law of God, and with flesh the law of sin.

I don't think it is any different for us today than it was for Paul in his day, as he concludes in verses 24 through 26, "Who can deliver me from this body of death—I thank God—through Jesus Christ our lord. With my mind, that is my spirit, I serve Christ our lord, but with my will my desire is to serve the flesh." [24] O wretched man that I am! Who will deliver me from this body of death? [25] I thank God—through Jesus Christ our Lord! So then, with the mind I myself serve the law of God, but with the flesh the law of sin.

I believe that without the Holy Spirit's guidance, no one can serve Jesus Christ or be drawn to him. For in my life, it has been my will not to follow Christ; I only follow him because of his spirit, which lives in me, and because before I knew Jesus Christ I desired nothing good, and now all I want is to be close to him and to be in his presence daily.

Human will is just that: man's will and not God's. And as Adam, the first man, desired to do evil, so do I. Now, the difference between Adam and me is that I have a replacement for my will, and he didn't. Whatever he willed was his conclusion, and even with an exterior helper, Eve, his heart was doomed because he wanted only to please his flesh; what comes from the earth always desires to return to it. Before God cursed the earth, man's will and God's were one. Afterwards, the only way man could defeat this interior helper—his will—was to turn back to the one who made it and him.

Without the Lord, there is no help for the will of man. As it was in the beginning, it is and will be in the end. God had to save man from his own will; the death of one man became the life of all men. It was the will of the first man (Adam) to disobey the God that created him, and it was the will of the second man (Jesus

Christ) to obey his God, who sent him as an example of a man who could control his own flesh and override human will. So what we celebrate as free will actually enslaves us to do evil. The will of man is not the will of God, or anything like it. Human will acts as if the flesh is its God; it wants only to obey what the flesh wants, and it does not desire the things of the spirit, for it is corrupt, seeing life through a gambler's eyes, always betting on the odds. Never following what is true and holy and simple, the way of the flesh is the way of man's will, for they agree, and one loves the other.

The only way man can avoid destruction by his own will is to surrender it to Jesus Christ. In doing so, he will be forgiven by the love of God, becoming a new creature through the process of regeneration, or being born again. Romans 10:9 tells us that if you confess with your mouth the Lord Jesus and believe in your heart that God raised him from the dead, you will be saved. The amazing thing is that being born again means having new spirit, not a new will. As I have stated before, if this will is separated from the spirit, it will kill, steal, and destroy. Evil does only what it has the power to do, so if it is my will to do good, it must be because of the goodness of God in me, grace extended to me by way of the cross.

Now that I have accepted Jesus Christ as my lord and savior, I can control my own will. Even when it wants to sin, I can stop it. When it wants to go against God's word or disobey his commandments, I can steer it to a safe harbor, away from where the seas toss and the harsh winds blow. This is my will: to do God's will. And now that Christ is the head of my life, it is easy for me to put my own will—the will of man—under subjection, walking with it instead of being led by it.

What is the will of man? I will explore two answers to this question: first, the will of man as his desire; and second, as his ability to do or not to do.

Let's look at human will as desire and explore whether it is even man's at all, or something altogether different than what we have come to believe, an innate command or power that tells all men what to do or not to do. Consider the word *desire*. Defined as such, human will simply comes down to whether we do or do not want something. The question is whether we have control over our own actions or something else has that control. We need to understand what is going on inside us, what we desire to do and not to do. Sometimes if given that choice, we choose wrong, and sometimes we choose right. So every time we come to a decision point, we should ask ourselves, *Is this the right thing to do?* What we have to remember is that the human will never corresponds with God's will, so we should not blindly go along with our own will. If it is not under the influence of the Holy Spirit, it will sin and possibly choose wrong. The only way for us to choose the right thing is to desire the right thing in the first place, and that must come from the spirit of righteousness inside us. We must have the same mind as Christ Jesus, a mind that desires to obey the father.

Desire means to long for, to want, or to wish to want. In Matthew 9:13 and 12:7, when Jesus quotes the Old Testament, saying, "I desire mercy, not sacrifice," he is not describing the father's perspective of what is truly important in our relationship with him. (See also Hebrews 10:5–8.) *The will of man is to seek what he wants to capture him. He seeks to be caught.* Sin is his greatest love. His mind forever seeks the pleasure of his flesh; the more his flesh eats, the more it wants. Human will does not desire life, only death. It has no thirst for righteousness, nor does it seek to do good, for to do wrong or bad gives it greatest joy.

I don't know why a just God would create an unjust will. But here is what I do know: it must have been to his liking, or else it would not be. As Sam Cook sang in his rendition of an old Negro spiritual, "We will all understand it better by and by."

THE HUMAN WILL

—according to Augustine and Pelagius

The British monk Pelagius and the North African bishop Augustine were contemporaries. They were both born in the fourth century A.D. Both claimed to be faithful teachers of the Bible.

In this article, I will specifically highlight their respective doctrine of the will, and show how it inevitably affected their doctrines of sin and grace.

The controversy between Augustine and Pelagius about man's will in his fallen condition was re-echoed a millennium later in Erasmus' Diatribe and Luther's answer in The Bondage of the Will. The able Reformer, like Augustine, knew from Scripture that sinful man has a will, indeed, but his will is enslaved and bent towards evil, and can do nothing except wickedness. For until man is converted, and

11

his will is renewed by the Holy Spirit, his will is captive to Satan, and "are taken captive by him at his will" (two Timothy 2:26).

Though the will is never forced, nor destined by any necessity of nature to perform evil, yet sinful man has lost all ability of will to perform any of the spiritual good, which accompanies salvation. He is not able, by an act of the will, to repent and believe on the Lord Jesus Christ. He is not willing to be converted. Jeremiah prayed, "Convert us, O Lord, and we shall be converted." Unless the Lord intervenes, man remains bound, for "the world loves darkness rather than light, because its deeds are evil" (Jn.3).

The natural man, according to Scripture (and Augustine), is altogether averse and opposed to spiritual good. Christ said, "You, being evil, are able to give good gifts to your children . . ." thus strongly emphasizing that our deeds, however bright and commendable, do not make us good in ourselves. A corrupt tree bears corrupt fruit. That is all it can do. The natural man is not able by his own strength to turn to God, or even dispose himself towards God (Titus 3:3-5; John 6:44). He is dead in sin (Ephesians 2:1-5). He is at enmity with God (Romans 5:6; 8:7).

Without a divine, gracious and radical renewal (accomplished in regeneration), man cannot fulfill any obligation to God. Grace is essential for man does not seek God. God seeks him.

Over against this, Pelagius asserted the full ability and potential in the human would. He taught that man could eliminate sin from his life by an act of the will. Man can keep the commandments of God, if he wants to. He reached this conclusion by twisted logic: "God would not command man to do what cannot be done by man." Thus Pelagius, in considering the will, forgot or rather played down the consequence of Adam's fall. Man was created able, but lost his ability through his apostasy. However, Pelagius asserted that no obligation could ever be placed outside man's limitless capacity for good.

How do these differing viewpoints affect the doctrines of sin and grace?

Evidently, for Augustine, if man has a perverse and wicked will, bound to sin, then we can see how sinful sin is, to what extremity sin has driven man. Man lost all knowledge of the true God, became guilty and sinful; he serves sin; all his faculties, including the will, are orientated towards the servitude of sin.

He does not want God; actually, he hates God and carves for himself a god in wood and stone or in this imagination.

Thus the will, directed against God, brings the most radical consequences. He has a corrupt nature from conception; he is under the influence of a prevailing effectual tendency to sin and wickedness.

What hope is there for man in such a state, being alienated from God by his willful ignorance "For though they knew God they did not glorify him . . . but became vain in the imaginations?" In such an enslavement, Augustine sees God's grace to be the only solution, the only remedy. God comes to man when man is fleeing from him. He does not force him to act against him will, but in grace renews his will. "I will remove the heart of stone and give them a new heart, that they may obey me . . ." (Ezek.). God's grace does not destroy freedom, for sinful man is far from being free. God's grace changes their will so that, once renewed, man freely chooses holiness rather than sin. "If the Son sets you free you shall be free indeed."

For Pelagius, his doctrine of man's wills is reflected (consistently enough) on his ideas about sin and grace. Pelagius taught that man's will, from birth, is a tabula rasa, neutral, neither sinful nor holy. It depends on man himself to use his will aright. Thus sin, for Pelagius, exists because we imitate the wrong doing of others. The sinner can overwhelm sin; it is not serious; it does not bring death.

Naturally, then, grace is nothing more than God's help. Man, according the Pelagius, is free to reject both the Law and the example of Christ. He can resist every inducement to follow Christ. Grace is clearly resistible for, as the poet Henley put it, "I am the master of my fate, the captain of my soul." I alone determine my destiny, my future, whether it will be blessed or miserable. Man can accept or reject proffered grace at will. Therefore, at the end of the day, man is his own Savior, for what determines his salvation is his will. (This Pelagian venom is common in Arminian circles today).

Thus we see how one heresy easily and naturally leads to another one for support. At least Pelagian system is consistent, consistently erroneous.

Augustine, having a viable anthropology (the constitution of man, including the nature of his will), see grace as the Only Rescue for enslaved man.

At the Council of Ephesus (431 A.D.) and the Synod of Orange (529 A.D.) Augustine was vindicated and Pelagius condemned. The system of Pelagius was shown to be erroneous and contrary to the Scriptures, while the Augustinian doctrine of sin and grace was approved (see further my article "What Orange decided").

Faithful brethren in Christ, is Augustine's position our firm belief? Alternatively, have we drunk from Pelagius' poison? Search and see . . .

I don't think we have drunk poison from some old man's cup of theological interpretation. But I do believe we are drinking the poison of every mild-mannered, neutral, lukewarm preacher, be it man or woman, who suggests that we can have a wonderful life if we just obey the simple law of believing in our own power: "If I believe it, I can do it or I can have it." This, too, sounds like Pelagius's system.

Before we go further into any thousand-year-old teaching, let's just see how toxic this type of thinking is. The problem today is that this type of thinking has engulfed the minds of new converts and caused a negative view of the true transformational process. To be a new creature, the transformed must have a transformer. New birth makes us children of God and leads to moral transformation, and I believe that it is this new mind that causes us to do right according to the word of God. For if we continue to do wrong, or we find that our flesh opposes the will of God, we have not experienced the new birth. If we have, the will of God replaces our will to sin, and we now wish to do good because he is in us. We cannot enjoy sin any longer once we eat of the fruit of God's love; it becomes *our* will to do God's will.

We must confess that our will is forever present, and in order not to be victimized by it, we must subject ourselves to what is true and holy and good. This can be done only after we, the sinners, come to the Son of God by way of grace. I will say that grace is not altogether understood in this context. Romans 6:14 tells us that grace releases us from the dominion of sin, so that we are not under the law, but under grace. In my own life, I have seen the spirit move in a fashion, as when folks pray for you even though you do not ask them to. I do believe it was that type of prayer that afforded me the opportunity to receive God's grace.

I know that Jesus's dying on the cross was not only an act of his obedience to his father's will and command, but also the act of grace itself. John 3 states it simply: God gave his only son to die for the world because the world could not die and redeem itself for Adam's sins. So Jesus's death is grace, the antidote to the death sentence we had because of our own will to sin against God. It was the prayers of the righteous received in heaven on my behalf that gave direction to the spirit of grace; by divine providence, grace goes after that soul closest to hell. It offers a clear-cut path—Jesus Christ—and if the sinner takes that path, he will not only find life, but find it in abundance.

What, then, becomes of the will of that man? As I stated earlier, it is now that man's privilege and pleasure to take what he did not earn and could not purchase by his own will. He did not desire Christ; it was Christ who desired him by way of Calvary, for if man could simply decide to do good, he would not have crucified an innocent man—he would have kept the laws of God without a blood sacrifice. Man can never do the will of God by his own will, for that will is evil and corrupt, averse to God and statutes and desiring only to do bad. With Jesus Christ as the head of your life, you will do good because it is the only thing Jesus knows to do. He even saved a murderer, an adulterer, a liar, a thief, a deceiver—every type of sinner.

We need to know that we don't come to God through our own will. Instead, it is because of our will that God comes to us. For man fell from the perfect love relationship that God had created for him when he made him, and everything in heaven and on earth knew that God desired to restore his relationship with man. God even arranged for the birth of his son to do job, because he had pursued man with every angel, saint, and prophet he could use to get that loving relationship back. It seems to me that God simply wanted to walk with man and talk to him again, for I believe God enjoyed the man more than the man enjoyed his God. I wish I could reverse the damage I did to my God by running away from him when all he really wanted was to love me, take care of me, and keep me in perfect peace. God, I am sorry for running away from you. I do not know why I ran away; all I know is that I did, and I ask your forgiveness.

We need only repent and ask for his forgiveness, and according to his word—and my life experience—he forgives in the greatest way. He restores you to your original position of being his child, no longer his enemy or a lost child. You get to be close to the God that made you, for that was the reason he made you: to glorify himself through you and to perfect you in his own perfect time. What a joy it will be to look in the face of God and see him smile because he has back what was his — and that, my friend, is you.

Who then would not obey a God like that? Yes, as good as he is, we still need to be reminded that if God is not the reason for our life and he does not speak through us, we will be controlled by that cursed thing, the human will that has plagued prior generations and will continue to plague generations to come. The will of man is like the Hindenburg. It flies around the world and acts as if nothing can hinder it, but the very name reflects its status: it is hindered in every way, and what it is made of — desires of the flesh, lust, imagination, all forms of explosive spiritual gas — will be its downfall or destruction. "Mega-church" pastors, TV ministers, radio preachers, and others like that make promises to people who believe their will for their own life is more powerful than God's will for their life. But promising a good life by the mere suggestion that it will happen is misleading. The belief that we can get everything we wish for simply by "willing" it has only led people to a more terrible state than the one they were in before. Consider the promise of winning the lottery: we know that the odds are millions to one, but we still try to be the one in the millions who wins the millions. For some strange reason we believe that if we will it, it will happen.

All too often we find that even the will to do something is not powerful enough to cause it to happen. So when we rely solely on our will, it does not do for us what we wanted it to do and does not produce a return on the request that we made of it. It just cannot do well on its own, even though we wish it would. So this will of ours is star-crossed, plagued by the Romeo and Juliet syndrome. To know love is to have death; to have your own will is to have it replaced by God's will. I believe God assassinates man's will with a double-edged sword, God's word, every time man invites him into his heart, because a perfect God cannot live in an imperfect heart. Maybe God is like an archer: he draws his bow and shoots through the heart with a precision that guarantees the death of the will. Like a man might shoot a clay disk for sport, God's bow propels the arrow of his holy spirit, which shatters man's will into millions of pieces, never to be put back together again. In its place is the spirit of God and the eternal desire to be like God and with him.

I can now understand Paul's conflict with his mortal body, and what it meant to him to have this thing to drag around and identify with (Rom. 7:24). He goes on to say in Romans 7:25, "With mind I myself serve the law of God, but with the flesh the law of sin." This flesh, too, is the downfall of many a good man, and I will forever keep in my mind that I am fully flesh and that, if I could, I would allow this flesh to reign supreme. But because of the law of God, I debate any decision before me, challenging myself to do not my will but what God wills for me to do. A good work may seem impossible to me, but to God it is possible. So I will to do God's will, and I trust that the word of God is my compass. Allowing it to lead me is the only way I can avoid the inevitable destruction that my will desires. I must retrieve the word of God from deep in my soul and be comforted knowing that if I follow it, everything will work out just fine.

My mind is parallel with this will, for it is always reminding me of the conflict between the two—the mind and the spirit—as if one needs to be better or stronger than the other. I often wonder if this conflict was meant to be, or if we just love to fight. Even if there is not a disagreement between our mind and spirit, we still may have two opinions, and when we give in to one or the other, we often find that it was our will that prevails.

I am so proud of my president and what he stands for. It was very moving and encouraging to see and hear his confidence and to know that the time is right for the truth, and that second place is not good enough for a genuine competitor. He spoke to the nation like a true president, saying something that we will hold onto and hope for: we now are ready to be a great nation again, to rip the reins from the hands of those who wish to take us backward. We need and now expect to be led into the long-awaited future, because we believe and look forward to that new and exciting change the president promised. And the same old ways of doing things will not suffice; the new ways, I hope, will be inspiring to those skeptics who only saw the glass as half full. I am glad to be back on the Obama train. It is good to believe in something and work toward it.

I can see very clearly that what a man wills, he can do, after he knows reason and truth. I still believe that the will of man is flawed and has no good intentions. But a man can have good intentions or the desire to do good, and he can reach a place where he is offered the opportunity to simply choose right or wrong. It is okay to make that choice once he is equipped with the ability to tell right from wrong. Only God has power over choice; we stumble at the crossroads and hesitate to choose either way, because we do not have the power to choose. Will is not just a matter of choosing, but also a matter of having the choices presented to us in the first place. I can see that human will is often most at peace when there is no choice before it. When there is no conflict, man's will is to continue the way it started or to take the easy way out. It appears to me that we wrestle with decisions only when we have to choose between right or wrong.

The will of man is manipulative and cunning. As an adjective, the word *cunning* means (1) **crafty and deceitful**—clever; artful in a way that is intended to deceive; (2) **cleverly thought out**—showing skill, shrewdness, and ingenuity in planning or doing something; or (3) **cute**—attractive in a pleasant and delicate way. As a noun, *cunning* means (1) **craftiness and deceitfulness**—the ability to deceive in a clever, subtle way; or (2) **skilled performance**—skill, ingenuity, or grace in doing something. The will of man seems to be all this and more. So to give credit to the true deceiver, we must first believe that it is just that: a deceiver. Human will is a deceiver on steroids, as cunning as a fox.

Jesus, our Lord and Savior, once called Herod a fox; I believe Jesus called Herod that because of his inner nature. As God in the flesh, Jesus was able to see into Herod's heart, into his spirit and his will. In Herod he saw the perfect example of human will: he desired not only to kill, but also to steal and to destroy. That's why Jesus called him by that name—not because the creation of the fox was a mistake, but because it was wrong for a human being to have the same nature as a common beast. When I read in the Bible that Jesus called this man by the name of an animal, it alarmed me for many reasons. But the main one is the remarkable parallels between the fox's behavior and Herod's. If we look closely at the character of the fox, we find that this animal tends to *steal, kill,* and *destroy. Steal*: According to Luke 3:18–20, Herod stole his brother's wife. *Kill*: Herod killed John the Baptist. *Destroy*: Herod destroyed everything he touched, including the mind of his brother's daughter, who asked for John the Baptist's head on a platter after performing a seductive dance for Herod at a party. The will of man has all these qualities, and if allowed to rule it will do the same: steal, kill, and destroy.

The way of man is the way of his flesh; if the flesh wants it, the will commands it and usually gets it. So to control this will is to control the man. Man must be separated from his will, and the only way he can have control is to have a will that will allow him that control, a new will that is not cunning in either sense. This opens the door to what I believe is one of the most horrific lies ever told to man: that he cannot have the will to do good all the time. It is inconsistent with the word of God for man to think he will forever be burdened with a will that is cunning and wants only to sin against God. I have myself as an example to thank. What has happened within me is nothing short of a miracle, for remember, my will was always to seek and do mischief, to lie, steal, and kill. As Paul says in the Book of Acts, I was a sinner among sinners, and my sins led to my confession. I am glad that God gave me the chance to verbalize this confession—I was a sinner and I loved it. Every wrong thing I ever did I enjoyed doing. God knows that my will was totally corrupt and forever deceitful.

My problem was the same as everyone's: I thought I could change myself. Especially when my sins got me into trouble with society and people saw me for what I really was, I was ashamed of myself and tried to stop my bad behavior. But I was never successful, and finally I just gave up and did what men often do when they can't find help: I turned to God. I am glad that God provided a way out for man, and I'll tell you, it really was a way out for me. My way out was what I call "the only way in," as one man ended and another began. Little did I know that this beginning would be a renewing, a new birth. I only knew that if I could just get rid of my desire to commit sin, if I no longer enjoyed sin, that would be great. So I surrendered to God, who captured me—and therein lay the beginning of a new person with a new mind, a new mind with the will to do good all the time.

I am stumped by the notion that God would give man only the desire and not the will to do good. For ever since I have had this new will, it has given me the power to choose a better way every time, not just sometimes. I dare not say that I have actually chosen the better way every time, but I stand by the truth that I at least have the strength to choose, when there was time when I could not and did not choose the right way.

Now I understand that time itself is of no help to man if his will is left in its natural state. *The Apostle Paul called it "the body of death," and I can and do agree: it's a dying, decaying thing.* I think the human will is as bad as evil itself, or at least it can destroy with same degree of impact on the human host that it burdens daily. If I could, I would relent from discussing this dreadful subject, but I must give at least as much attention to the human will as it gives to man, knowing that we should gain an understanding of the truth so it can guide us. This will is nothing less than a murderer. It has and will forever collaborate to do wicked work and seek to complete that work in every man. If only we were wise to this demon-driven spiritual wrecking ball, which smashes to pieces everything it hits. God gives all of us an understanding of right and wrong, and when we acknowledge that a thing is wrong, all we are doing is giving way to that fact—it's good to know, but choosing right over wrong is the greater problem, and that is where our human will fails us every time. It is zero out of a hundred. So I thank God for allowing me to see wrong and do right.

When a person stands by and watches another person mistreated, that is man's will at work. When a person sees another person mistreated and he or she intervenes, that is God's will at work. Consider the familiar passage of scripture in which Jesus tells the story of the Good Samaritan. When a man was left by robbers to die in a ditch, several people passed him by and did nothing to help him, even though they saw that he was in distress. I consider this a perfect expression of the will of man: although he sees and knows the right thing to do, he always chooses the wrong thing. Now let's take a look at the one man who chose to do God's will in his behavior toward the victimized man.

In Jesus's parable, a Samaritan man was traveling by, saw the fellow in the ditch, and noticed that he needed immediate help. He quickly gathered his strength and went into the ditch to retrieve the man. He set the man on his beast, took him to the nearest inn, and paid for his care and recovery. This scene paints a good picture of God's will in action. The contrast between the Samaritan and the other travelers is no accident. Christ does not tempt man to sin just to show him the sin that is already in him—the will of man and all that goes along with it.

Man's will also fails him when it comes to trust and reliability. Although a man may present himself as an honest being, when it comes to getting what he wants he is often manipulative and cunning. This will is of man is clever; it has devious ways of controlling or influencing someone—in most cases its own host—to get its own way or lead to some form of destruction. It is also deceitful and crafty, which means clever or artful in a way that is intended to deceive. It's at its best is when it is "attractive in a pleasant, delicate way." The will of man has the ability and the skill to deceive in a clever, subtle way—it simply fools you. I believe the human will is the primary factor that keeps man from turning to God, for it knows its own destiny and purpose, and if for one moment it relaxes its grip on the mind of man, it will be recognized as the deceiver it is.

God made this will not to hinder man, but to give himself glory when and if man, who was created in his own image, overcomes the will that resides within him. Though the victory is his, he still must say no to that which is most familiar to him, which walks with him every day of his life, just as Judas walked with Jesus. The will of man itself cannot please God or man. It only wants to please its own appetite, and that is the lust of the flesh and the imagination. If we knew the true intent of our will, we would not give in to it; we would control it instead of it controlling us. I believe that for one to truly know himself, he must first know his will, for the will, if it's allowed to, will misrepresent itself as the person. I have found that the real person is not represented by the will. The real person is in his soul, not his will. According to God, man was originally a three-fold being, but he now is seen as a single being by way of his soul. Because of that, the least part of the three is now the true representative of all three parts. The greatest known battle of man against his own soul was the battle fought by Jesus Christ on the cross. I thank God, my father in heaven, for now I know that it wasn't only Adam that fell in the Garden; it was his will, also. Adam didn't realize that he had been deceived not by Eve, but by his own will, so he could not answer his God.

This is the same problem we are having today: when we sin we are not even aware of the inner workings of our will, so we usually blame failure on external forces, someone or something else. We never take the time to examine the status of our own hearts to see if the will of God is present there, or whether it is still our will in charge. I have to accept that when my will is in charge, I always lose, and when the Lord's will is in charge, I always win. I am often asked how we can know who is in charge of our soul, and how we can recognize when a change has happened. For me, the answer is very simple: When man decides anything without the total leadership of God, his decision is always flesh-related and lust-based. But when God is controlling his decision, it is always love-based, guided by the Holy Spirit.

Whenever there is a conflict between man and God it almost always results in man realizing that he is wrong and God is always right. The will of man is forever flawed and cannot be saved. A man's soul is the only part of him worth saving, so the soul must be offered up to God, who will replace man's will with his own. Then the newly recreated man will obey the

Lord, and the satisfaction of pleasing God will forever be his reason for life: simply to give God glory and stand before God's marvelous design.

Man's soul versus his will offers the most embarrassing contrast of characters—one I often compare to Dr. Jekyll and Mr. Hyde. For it seems as if Mr. Hyde, the brute of the two, wants only to kill, steal, and destroy, embarrassing the doctor. When Dr. Jekyll suppresses him or keeps the brute under control, his life is almost always pleasant. We are never too far away from our own will, just as Dr. Jekyll, whenever he looks in the mirror, see the brute along with himself. There is no way to escape the presence of human will. It's always there. The only thing a man can do is understand the character of his will and control its behavior by replacing it with the will of God, much as we wear clothes to protect us from the elements, even though we have hair on our body. Our natural protection is inadequate and can be improved upon. In the same way, the will that we inherited from Adam, the first man, was improved upon with Jesus Christ, the second man. Jesus not only became a friend to man, but he also *was* man, the man that God had originally called "good," not the man that ate the apple. So the only way for man to escape the embarrassing outcome of his own will is to allow Christ to replace Adam's nature with his nature.

I can personally agree with the famous passage in Matthew 46:21: "The spirit is willing, but the flesh is weak." It might seem as if Matthew is using the word *flesh* to describe the will of man, but that's not the case. While there are some similarities, the flesh will obey the law of survival, trying to live even if it must resort to cannibalism. When it does not get food or water, it will use its reserves to survive. But man's will does not have any reserves. It has no means of storing anything, for to preserve would facilitate life, and it only knows the skill of causing death. It is the beast that lives within us, and it has an appetite for flesh and soul. It does not quit until it has destroyed its host, just like a cancerous tumor that grows bigger and bigger until the body dies and the tumor no longer has anything to feed on. Much as fungus grows on a tree, so does the will of man grow on an unprotected heart, smothering it subtly until it is allowed to fully guide and control the person's daily life. I have noticed that when a man surrenders to his will, he often gives way to the sins of the world without even questioning whether they are leading him to destruction or death. He trusts his will because it seems right at the time. But experience has proven that man's will always leads him to certain death. It causes him to break and violate God's will, and Jesus himself said that "the wages of sin is death."

The will of man offers futility at best. It works in every possible way to oppose God's commandments. It prefers witchcraft over praise and worship. It prefers homosexuality over the marriage of a man and a woman. It prefers sickness over health. It prefers sadness over joy. It prefers night over day.

This will is an aftermarket product rather than an original from the maker. It could be seen as the scar tissue from Adam's wounded ribcage, a perversion of Adam's jealous mind, which believed that every fruit should be his to consume. The will made its case that maybe God would relent, and Adam gave in to it. The reason for that failure will forever be a mystery. God only knows why a man who had everything lost it all and never saw it coming. I do believe that if Adam had known he was being misled, he would have stopped his will in it tracks and thereby saved his own life, because it is obvious that he had a choice. He chose the lesser of the two options.

It is now clear that when we come to a crossroads in life, we should take time to reflect on the road that led us to that point. If we find that our journey has been full of deception, lies, murder, or robbery, it might just be that what has led us thus far should not assist us in choosing the road ahead. At any of life's crossroads, we never know how much time we have left to travel—and how sad it would be to find ourselves in the last days or moments of life, realizing that all we needed to do was choose the righteous path. That will of ours always and forever says, *Go left! Go left!*—knowing that as soon as we turn that way, death will receive us.

I tell you that the will of man should not be trusted. It should not be confused with God's will, for when the will of man is given the opportunity to choose for us, we lose. God has already given his life for us by way of his son, that we can have life, and have it more abundantly. To all who have been saved by the shedding of the blood of Jesus Christ on Calvary, I say that your salvation was the will of God, not the will of man. The whole work of salvation relies on God's will, for it was and is impossible for man to die for his own sins, and I have never met a man who had the will to do so even if he could. Again I say that man's will is to destroy, not to make whole; to die in shame, not to be raised in glory. And at all times we should remember that Jesus Christ is replacing the will of man daily.

That's why Paul said, "I die daily" — the transforming mind is one that is always dying, giving way to a new mind. The new mind is the new will, and the new will is the will of God. If we lose our will, it is good, for then and only then can we receive God's will.

My fate is not the same as my will, for it is the will that I cannot control, but my fate is always subject to God's word. So if I do not do God's will, then my fate is not that of God's word, but if I do what is God's will for my life, then my fate is according to his will. Even before he gave me life, he ordained me to give him glory through my life, so it pleases me to know that when I obey him, I please him. We must always remember that it was God that took the first step, not man; therefore it is still God, not man, who has the first and last word.

I often wonder why God did not leave David in his sinful condition when he fell from grace. After all, it was David who chose to sin; it was not God's will that David sin or break his covenant with God. So I do believe that God could have allowed him to perish in that very act of sin. The Lord didn't punish David as he did the Hebrews who made a calf in the desert, instantly killing thousands of them and saving only those who chose to follow him through Moses (Exod.

32:1–35). Whatever his reasons, I am very sure of one thing: if and when we are sentenced to die because of our sins, it is God's call whether to carry out that sentence. The Bible provides us evidence of God's will, and for that reason we should always give way to that will, because it offers total grace and complete mercy. We need not be confused—it is God's will alone that is good, and man cannot be and never has been good. Even Solomon, with all his wisdom, could not do a good deed by his own will alone. If he made a judgment, it was because God gave him the wisdom to do it. And when Paul made the decision to live for Jesus, it was not that he was a good man doing a good thing; he simply accepted the goodness of God and would forever try to repay him by giving everything he had and everything he knew to the cause of spreading the Gospel. And when he finished his course of life, he finished well, because he realized then more than ever that it was the will of God, not his will, that he give his life for the Gospel. By way of the Holy Spirit, God guided Paul from blindness to light, and he could forever see.

That is why the word of God is the only tool that can help man understand his own will. For by the word, man can see his shortfalls—and we have too many to count. But through these shortfalls we find in the most humbling way that we need Jesus to find us, for without him we are lost and cannot find our own way. We need him to show us the way, and we need him to *be* the way. Once man understands that, he will see that his own will is his enemy. It is not his mind or his flesh, but the beast that's trying to kill his flesh and destroy his mind. It is no less than the devil, an inspiring evil that lives within and without, made manifest in everything he does. We are able to withstand the wiles of the will of man and the wiles of the will of the devil only if we first submit to the will of God.

God gave man license to choose who would lead and guide him for the remainder of his life, and whoever he chose would be his master. Even though we cannot choose our earthly father or mother, we do have the blessing of being able to choose our father in the spirit while we are on this earth—and that's where we have a life-and-death decision. If we choose God (Jesus), we live forever. If we choose any other god, we die now and forever. Jesus speaks of this life-or-death choice at least twice in the New Testament, saying that if we choose the devil, we then belong to him. In John 8:42 he tells the children of the devil, "If God were your father, you would love me, for I came from God and now am here. I have not come of my own." And in

John 8:44 he tells them, "You belong to your father, the devil, and you want to carry out your father's desire . . . for there is no truth in him. When he lies, he speaks his native language, for he is a liar and the father of lies." The will of your master will be done on earth as it is in heaven—or hell.

I am proud to say that I have totally surrendered to God and his will, and because of that decision I can say I expect to receive the glorious blessing of eternal life. And as I have already secured it through the gift of God's grace, this new life came by way of a new will.

Simply hoping for something better is traditionally the way we believe that it will come, and so whatever we receive is exactly what we deserve—that is, the faith we have in something often can be seen in the results. The truth is, we shouldn't expect any more than the effort we put out. It is becoming very clear that a whole generation of believers was fooled into thinking that their lives would be changed by the process of giving to some ministry or religious leader. Sad as it is, no one came to these people's rescue. Harvard, Yale, Duke, UCLA—no institution of higher education said anything about what these "religious" leaders were doing to the minds of God's children. It was as if they were left in a cage with hungry lions. And now their lives are torn to pieces, and the great hope of getting all the things they were once promised will never be realized.

That's what I notice when it comes to the human will: it leads man to believe in a lie and then never explains how or why the lie came about. The will can have such a devastating effect on the human psyche that when these religious parties were found to be wrong, the people who were preyed upon still would not believe the evidence of their predators' wrongdoing, becoming willing victims. Their will was so strong it seems as if they would have drunk poison had they been asked to do so. (Remember Jim Jones?) The will of man has a very strong influence on his mind. It can prevent the mind from doing anything, so that even rational thought is elusive. The man may feel as though no harm is being done, but he fails to see that the very act of doing nothing is a type of destruction that will eventually cause a state of lethargy, and an eventual wasting away. Man cannot trust the old saying that "emptiness means opportunity," because in some cases emptiness means that final destruction has taken place, with nothing left to follow. Consider the story of the great entertainer Michael Jackson. The theme of his last public appearances—through video, album, and concerts—was "This is it." And indeed we soon discovered it was "it," the last moments of his life. It was his choice to do the things he did, and ultimately all the decision he had made, made him. And it really was "it," *the end*.

It is as if a tornado has swept the land clear by way of a flood. Everything has been washed away—*everything*—and there is nothing to rebuild with. All that is left is grief. The truth is, once the human will has its way with the human mind, man will die, and nothing can save him from that promised death, not even God. As we are told in 1 Samuel 8:18, "When that day comes, you will cry out for relief from the king you have chosen, and the lord will not answer you in that day." When we do not choose Jesus, we have already chosen another god, and that god is now our king. It was God who pronounced this death in the first place. To give himself glory, he will not fail on any promise he makes, so we are not too far from our own destruction. We have a will that is averse to God's will, so it is necessary for us to understand that unless we are born again, we cannot avoid the trickery of the will we were born with. The scriptures tell us that one man brought sin into the world (Romans 5:12: "Wherefore, as by one man sin entered into the world, and death by sin . . ."). And so I am pleased to say that when a man learns that he has a problem that he cannot resolve himself, he must turn to Jesus, the only one who can replace the will that he inherited from the flesh of Adam.

God did not give man a flaw or a sin. Man gave that to himself with his decision in the Garden. He had a choice, and he made that choice as soon as he desired something different than what God wanted for him. Man's will inspired evil and encouraged God's adversary, Satan, who showed man how beautiful the fruit was and told him that he hadn't entirely understood God's words. Man simply fell for the trickery, reached out his hand, took the fruit, and ate it. He wanted to choose another way, and he did. God did not punish himself for man's failure; he punished man, because it was man who sinned, not God. God knew that Satan was trying to persuade the mind of man, just as he had persuaded the mind of the angels. They, too, had a will, and it fooled them into following Satan's will to oppose God, the creator.

Is this now happening to man? Are we willing ourselves to oppose God, and will we be punished like the angels? We can use our will to turn to Jesus and receive forgiveness, and God will give us a helpmeet or a comforter to keep us safe from our own will. He will simply think for us, giving us divine guidance so that every problem becomes transparent, every choice or decision becomes easier to decide, and everything becomes clearer. We need not see through a dark glass when our eyes have been washed by the blood of Jesus. I am glad that I can see and that the world holds no more secrets for me. The Holy Spirit has given me the advantage. I know it not fair. But that's the way it is, and the truth is that life is not fair, either, and over time it's been proven that with Jesus, we win.

I often think that if it were not for human will, man would live a longer life. Let me explain what I mean. When we are left with our own will, we are always thinking of something to do with our hands or our minds, so that we never rest. Most of the time, though, our activities are unproductive — we're simply burning the candle at both ends, and we burn out more quickly than we would have if we were not so busy. The less stressed we are, the more life we live. As I, Johnny Rutledge, always say, "Life is as it is, and we must live it." It's my will to live that kind of life, but there goes man, following his own will, trying to understand it, which is unusually taxing. It is my desire to do God's will, and this book is, to me, a manifestation of his will, a summary of all the reasons I can come up with for the way things should be.

The sole purpose of the will of man is to choose God and give him glory. I have found that the way to God's heart is to give him glory with your life and make the best out of your life. Often we are confused about human will, because everyone who has written about it explains it in the context of God's will. They can't understand how we can put our own corrupt spirit next to the perfect will of God—we are not even worthy to refer to the two in the same sentence. Man's will is bad, while God's will is good; man's will is doomed, while God's will is forever. There is no similarity between the two.

In some states of mind, your human will can cause you much harm or pain. First there is the problem that you're in a state of sin and don't want to stop that sin. When that happens, you have no sense of remorse, and your human will even assists you in the sin by telling you that it's okay, what's done is done, and you are all right. It does not care if someone else was hurt or destroyed by your sin; it acts as if you wanted to be a bad person all along, encouraging you to make one excuse after another for your bad behavior so that you can choose to do whatever you want and feel no shame. That's why we continue to sin publicly. A lot of people all over the world are doing things they should not be doing, publicizing all kinds of behaviors that they are not ashamed of. They simply don't care what anyone thinks about their image or actions; they just say it's their thing and they can do whatever they want. They will do what they want to do, even if someone else disapproves or gets hurt. And after all the damage is done, the human will affords man the privilege of having no guilt; it just tells him that at the end of the day, whatever happened is past and we are not to talk about or even remember it. In that way he is led to believe that he holds no responsibility for his behavior, so he has nothing to feel guilty about. The will of man has a clear message: Out of sight, out of mind. That's the way it always is when man's will is in charge of his life.

I denounce this will, which has caused me to suffer poor behavioral control. People have different interpretations of the concept of free will, but I know that I cannot control this will. I have found that when we give in to it, we give in to the least of ourselves. What I now know is that the will makes us very conscious of what we expect for ourselves. It will not be silent about a like or desire; instead, it yearns for attention and always wants to be in control. If I could describe my will, it would be like this: out of control, mad at the world, indifferent to real-life situations, aggressive, always wishing to be in charge, excited, and depressed. My attitude has two speeds—the first is "all out," and the second is no movement at all.

The will of man should never be overlook or allowed to continue on its own momentum without being checked daily. You should regularly examine it to see if you are in complete agreement with its activity. If allowed to go unchecked, it will lead you to one of three destinations: first, to steal (breaking God's law); second, to destroy (through divorce or other family destruction); and third—last but not least—to kill (removing the possibility of life altogether).

At some point we need to open our minds to the fact that we do have a will that is separate from our soul and body. Even if we don't believe it, we already will have given it total control over our lives, which spells disaster. The human will always desires more and more, so even if we are satisfied, it does not agree with the true needs of the body or soul; instead it feeds its cravings. The body always wants to eat and sleep more than anything else, and when your will has control over your body, it allows your body to do so in excess. For instance, if it wants to eat more than the stomach can handle, the will allows it to do so with no regrets. When the body wants to sleep, the will simply tells it to sleep as long as it wants to and not to worry about life, which will take care of itself. So the will leads the person into negligence, irresponsibility, unaccountability, and finally depression.

The concept of "the gift of choice" strikes a strange chord in my heart. I have come to believe that choice is a means of imprisonment, keeping true liberty at bay. I often see myself as a single entity with one mind, one self, or one voice, and that is always the case. The reason I feel that way is that I don't want to accept the part of me that always causes me the most problems—the inner man, or the thing that I call the will, which, if I let it, will always cause me to cater to my flesh. For some reason that will came to me when I was a very small child, and it has not left yet, some fifty years later. I would totally understand it if it were something I could see and touch, but therein lies my problem: it is elusive. Like a chameleon, it matches whatever situation it finds itself in, camouflaging itself to look like me. The only positive thing about this will of mine is that it always desires the same things. It never changes—it is a dependable negative. I wish that I were not ashamed of the behavior it causes; maybe then I would entertain it more, just to get a better understanding of it. The truth is that it only wants to be pleased and to please this flesh. As a child I would always wonder why I had to cater to the flesh, and why I had to have fleshly feelings. Lo and behold, I discovered that it was not just me; everyone was going through this and trying to make sense of it.

Man's will controls the part of him that wants to entertain the flesh in any capacity. It's as if man needs a guide, even if this guide leads him to some form of destruction, and even though when he gets to where he is going, he only then finds out that he has been misled. So I am convinced that this will is no more man than man is his will. In order to always see the truth of the matter, I must now the face the facts: the will is man's first enemy, and this will was created by God himself. God alone should be blamed for our great gift of choice, a pleasure we have because of this will.

Whether it's now or later, we will have to choose whether or not to obey our will. It cannot stand in awe of the very man it commands daily; it must simply give orders, like a general on a battlefield. The problem with this battle is that the same general who commands the man is also the enemy the man must fight—and that's when this becomes his daily war. If man could have one day of respite from this enemy, I do believe he would find rest and maybe some form of peace. As it says in the What is man that You are mindful of him, Bible, "What is man that thou are so mindful of him?" I believe that if this very same angel had thought to choose his words more carefully, he would have said something like this: "What is this creature that you have created, that you have given it a free will to make daily choices? This man has conflict in his design, and because of that conflict, he cannot be seen as a perfect creation. The very gift of choice is the curse that becomes his will, and daily he fights this war in his head." I suspect that the angels do not envy man as we may think they do. They simply pity us, for unlike us, they always know exactly what they will and will not do at every moment. Those that keep their mind on the Lord will stay in perfect peace, and those that keep their mind on evil are at peace, also, but they know that their final destination will be total destruction, because they have chosen that fate. We do the same thing daily, but because of grace we get a new dose of willpower to do either good or bad with the same gift of choice. That can make for a good creation or a confused creation, a good or a not-so-good man.

The will of man will always be his shepherd, urging him forward to climb this hill or to cross this river or to run this race. Even if he does not win, he must still compete. My point is clear: without his free will, man would not be any more or less than any other of God's creations, because to be a human being, one must always be a human *doing*. Because of his humanity, man always has a choice before him, to do or not to do—and even if he chooses to do nothing at all, he still has made a choice. And he makes each choice because he wills it to be. The will is reflected in the choice, and it not always clear if it is the will of man or the man that wills. However, we must face the truth that the will of man is the same today as it was yesterday and as it will be forevermore: it always wants man to make a choice, which leads him to another place of choice, and another, so that the human will has its way with man in the end. What I have learned is that even with such great influence, the will still belongs to the very man it commands daily. When man accepts the fact that this will is present and a part of his creation, he can begin to control it and use it to better his life and reshape his destiny.

It appears to me that the human will is self-destructing, a vehicle that's always headed for a crash. Man's failures are always a direct result of his will; he simply wills them to be and will not have it any other way. Now, man has the God-given right to use his will—that's not the argument. The problem is with what he wills. I believe that if man were left without choices or the ability to choose, he would simply flow downwards, like water flows through a trench. God doesn't make man believe he has everything he needs, just in case he wishes to think for himself. The will of man is in no way attached to God, and it can never be, because God cannot sin or make mistakes, and the will of man is a sin itself. That is why it has destroyed man's total existence from the beginning, when Adam became its first victim. Adam chose the wrong way—he willed it to be—just as Jesus willed it to be that man could be saved and have eternal life by choosing Jesus Christ as his savior. There must be a reason why some people find this task too great and never make that choice. It is man's will that keeps him from choosing Jesus Christ to be his God; he simply wills it not to be.

I often ask myself why God did not remove Satan's influence on man's will. If man had not been influenced by the enemy, he would have chosen the right way, because there would be no other way to choose. In other words, no devil, no choice: it would be God and God alone that we would see. The truth is that when man gets so far gone he cannot even see the other side, he often sticks with what is convenient. So if we were born into sin and that is all we know, that will be all we look forward to, and we'll come to believe that there is no other way to be. The question is, why does man desire to do things that harm him, and what drives him to do them? I will try to answer this way: man is not his own creation. He did not make himself. His earthly desires are all a part of his lust, and his lust comes from the very flesh he is adorned with. For instance, if a man dresses like a clown, he will be seen as a clown and not as a man. The flesh is better left in its natural state so that it does not fool its own host. The term *white-collar crime* was coined because the men who committed those crimes wore white collars. The collars were clean and white, yet they did not and could not prevent the men wearing them from committing the crimes. The will of those men wearing those white collars caused them to commit black, dirty crimes.

I really believe that the only way man can escape the overpowering force of his own will is to counter it with the will of God. Jesus Christ demonstrated the perfect will of God by living every day of his life without sin and never letting the flesh control him. Even though we will never reach perfection on earth, as he did, we can and should have power over our flesh. We can simply will it to be. The flesh is not our God; it is our body. And the matter it is composed of is not more powerful than our mind. The mind tells the body what to do. If we make an effort to control this body, it will obey every command we give it, including the command to do nothing. We simply tell our hands to grab, and they do so without asking why. The human mind should not take vacations. It should always be alert and on the job, because in some situations the body or the flesh reacts to things without warning or even reason—it just does what it does. After all, that is all it knows how to do—be flesh—until the mind tells it something different. We give too much credit to this flesh, often ignoring the motivation behind the feelings we have, as though the feelings themselves validated the motivation. On the contrary, the feelings are irrelevant; the motivation must support the intent. (Man cannot stay in a place where if he feels like doing something, he does it. For example, today I felt like running outside in the park, but because it was dark and dangerous, I decided not to do it, even though I thought about it.)

So I ask myself, *What is this thing inside me that I now understand to be my will—and if it is my will, what part of me is it?* These questions always give me pause, simply because I can't see why my mind is not the only mechanism that controls all of me. The reason we need to get a better handle on our human will is that it does not seem to respond to current situations or life changes. It only wants what it wants *when it wants it,* and it was designed not to compromise, but to succeed, without concern for the final state of the person over which it has total control. If God had made this will to be submissive, it would have had to obey man. The only time in my life I had control over my will is when I took it by force. I had to take over my life with my mind, telling my will that I would not allow it to destroy me. But it was always positioned to take back control, and if I had allowed it to, it would have returned to its original purpose of leading me away from the righteousness of God.

The truth about the will of man is that it has always been his downfall, and until he recognizes its existence, he will have no control over it. Given the chance, it would destroy the very man it possesses. It seems to me that the will of man is just like any other creation that God gave man dominion over, yet it is in man, part of the whole man. When I look at human history and behavior and wonder how man could have been so evil, I know that it wasn't always a matter of the evil in man; sometimes it was a matter of the will of man, desiring to do evil. This will was what Paul called the "body of death," which forever plagued him and from which no one could separate him. It was clear to Paul, but I don't think it is clear to man, that this will is like an animal. It has its claws in its host, and everywhere it goes it hangs on for dear life. Paul could not shake it loose, and neither can we. It is our sin as flesh. It is the will of man that causes him to overdo everything he does. Man would literally destroy his home, his community, even his entire world if he allowed his will to have its way. The amazing thing about this will is that it has nothing to lose. After all, it is only the will of man, not *the* man.

I often wonder why we were given the problem of choice. If we must have choice, we should at least have the wisdom to make the better one, life instead of death. We cannot truthfully say that we are free to choose when we always make choices that bind and imprison us. When we choose life, we choose the creator of life, Jesus Christ. Even before we learned of this eternal blessing, we were given grace until we found out about it. I am so glad that my salvation is not a footrace between the devil and me. It was always available, although I had to choose it—and my will was *not* to accept this gift. My soul needed a break from the tired search for comfort and peace. As it was, nothing satisfied my soul until I received the love that Jesus Christ gave me when I accepted him as my lord and my God. Then I noticed an instant change inside me. Now I rejoice in knowing that he saved me by dying on Calvary, bearing the cross for every sinner. If we believe in this sacrifice, we are instantly rewarded with gift of eternal life. Yes, it is true: God removes the punishment of death.

"The mind is a terrible thing to waste." I used to hear that cliché and never wonder about its meaning, but now that I am older and have seen so many who have lost their mind, or appeared to do so, I realize that the mind reflects the activity of the soul. Man needs a new mind in order to have the peace he seeks, for the mind has just as much to do with decision making as the will does. What I have learned is that the will never takes a break. It is always on the job, and it has the only tool that can cause the mind to act out: a thought. As a man thinks, so he is. A thought may not cause an external action every time, but in general, the mind thinks, the body obeys, and the soul pays. Remember Isaiah 26:3: "Thou will keep him in perfect peace whose mind stay on thee because he trusts in the lord." This verse assures us that if a man keeps his mind on the Lord, he will have total control over his will, and the word of God will guide him through all life's challenges. Or as it says in Romans 14:5, "Let every man be fully persuaded in his own mind." The mind has every skill necessary to manage a man's willpower, and if the mind is convinced, it can direct the will by its decisions. If a man's mind is led by the word of God, his will reflects God's mind. But if a man's will is allowed to rule over the mind, it will destroy the man. It simply cannot be left to its own means. In its natural state, man's will is to oppose the will of God and destroy its host, which is man.

I don't quite understand why God would design man in this fashion, knowing even before his birth that as soon as he takes his first breath, he will desire the opposite of what God wants for him. It is very fitting that God would give man this thing called "free will" and then watch him make the wrong choices all his life. I think that man finally realizes that the ability to choose is not altogether a good thing when he has made major mistakes—then he turns to the Creator for true guidance. Once man trusts that God will lead him for the rest of his life, his will becomes an asset to him instead of a burden. It is a great joy to discover that even though the will can be the very thing that destroys a man, it is also the thing that can save him from destruction. This is something every man must discover in his own life: he must learn during the journey in order to stay on the journey. The races we run in life are never really finished; as soon as we cross one finish line, the next race starts. Every accomplishment gives birth to a new challenge.

Once man detects and accepts his will, he must immediately educate his mind and recognize the will for what God said it is: the privilege of having a choice. And the truth of the matter is that when man chooses, it is his God-given right to do so, and regardless of whether the choice is good or bad, it remains his choice. If he appreciates the privilege, he will always come back to the one who gave him the choice in the first place. We should never forget that the mind is not place of inactivity — it was and always will be a place of activity. Everything we know came from the mind of man, and God communicates that knowledge by way of the mind of man. God created man's mind so that it always desires more knowledge and yearns for more information, and then he made the mind to act according to its own capacity. If it agrees with its own design, it will learn relentlessly; if it does not, it will continue on its normal route. And if the opportunity presents itself, the mind in some cases will overrule itself and do nothing. That happens when man becomes stalled and does not even dream. At this point little growth takes place; he's simply standing still, with a lazy mind and slow blood. His human will is no help when this happens.

In fact, it guides man into this unproductive state, as it is always in agreement with the destruction of man altogether. The man will find a different route only when he hears a voice other than the one in his head. It is then that he will be given knowledge that will lead him back to the place of decision making.

Along with knowledge, man was also given the will to choose, and that could always be seen as a right, not a rule. We'll never totally understand how the mind can completely comprehend the right choices yet always choose the wrong choice. If man has the knowledge to make the right choice, why can't he do so? It is at this point that the great battle begins: the battle of man's will versus his mind. I do believe that if the mind were allowed to operate on its own, without the will trying to steer it in another direction, it would choose the right thing daily. But herein lies the problem: the first law of nature is self-preservation, and both man's will and his mind are trying to survive, each wanting to usurp the other. Only the heart can supersede both with ease. It always gets my attention when I see this drama played out. It is as if this war of wills is a star-crossed affair, and the heart sits on the sidelines, awaiting its chance to enter into the fight—not with the intention of fighting, but of separating the two foes in the hope that the mind will see the better approach to solving the problem. The heart is the soul of man, and it can act only according to what it is composed of. It is a blank canvas until the first thought enters into it, and then it's turned on for all eternity—every word and thought a man has from that point on is recorded in it. That is where the great war of wills longs to be. The one that controls the greater part of the soul is the one that has the most influence over it, and the one that possesses a man's soul will be the controlling factor in the war and will be rewarded control over its rival. A man's will must not win this war, or we will witness his final destruction. The mind is a terrible thing to waste, especially if it does not know that it will soon be destroyed, along with the man it possesses. It is not altogether good that the mind has been given such confidence, that simply because it is in charge, it will do what is right for the man. A good mind is one that does good for the man and mankind. A bad mind is one that does bad for the man and mankind.

The will of man was given to him by God, and yet it is forever wicked. It cannot be good, for it is the enemy of God. But left in its state of just being a will, it can do no harm. The place where it intersects with the will of the mind is where it gets the chance to control the mind, and unless the mind is full of knowledge of something greater, it will give way to a weaker will. The mind must always be in pursuit of more knowledge, and it must equip itself with the *right* knowledge according to its environment. For instance, if a person lives in Alaska, his mind must learn every detail about cold weather and how to survive in cold weather. Even if the body cannot recognize the danger of the freezing weather, the mind must override it and try and convince it to take shelter or it will die. The will to live will be evident only when the mind takes over and the person is spared from that horrible fate. The will of man is in direct contrast with this behavior, often leading to sad results. It may let the man freeze to death and yet convince him that that's the way it should be, that he should simply allow nature to take its course. The will of man will tell him that it's all right to die, that the death won't really be death, but a new beginning . . . it's amazing the simple approach that the will can take in its deceit. But the true picture becomes quite different if the man freezes to death; his life is over, the lives attached to his is over, and the lives attached to theirs is over, too. So man must continue to live, even if the outlook is grim. He must never surrender to the will to die, but always give way to his mind's will to live. And through his effort, life will always find a way.

The most important thing about the will of man is that it has no time frame. It is there whether you know it or not, and it will destroy you whether you know it or not. It simply has its own objective—to kill, to steal, and to destroy its own host. When the Apostle Paul spoke of the will of man, he drew a conclusion that is as true today as it was in his day: what a man wills is supreme to what the mind desires. Consider Paul's words in Romans 7:13–25, which begins with his pictorial description of a man's will fighting against his mind. As Paul presents it, man's will is the sin that fights against the will of the mind, which is man's integrity:

Has then what is good become death to me? Certainly not! But sin, that it might appear sin, was producing death in me through what is good, so that sin through the commandment might become exceedingly sinful. But we know the law is spiritual and I am carnal, sold under sin. For what I am doing I do not understand, for what I will to do, I do not practice; but what I hate that I do. If then, I do what I will not to do, I agree with the law that it is good. But now it is no longer I who do it, but sin that dwells in me. For I know that in me (that is, in my flesh) nothing good dwells; for to will is present with me, but how to perform what is good I do not find. For the good that I will to do, I do not do; but the evil I will not to do, that I will practice. Now if I do what I will not do, it is no longer I who do it, but sin that dwells in me. I find then a law, that evil is present with me, the will to good. For I delight in the law of God according to inward man. But I see another law in my members, warring against the war of my mind, and bringing me into captivity to the law of sin which is in my members. O wretched man that I am! Who will deliver me from this body of death? I thank God—through Jesus Christ our lord! So then, with the mind I myself serve the law of God, but with the flesh the law of sin. [13] Has then what is good become death to me? Certainly not! But sin, that it might appear sin, was producing death in me through what is good, so that sin through the commandment might become exceedingly sinful. [14] For we know that the law is spiritual, but I am carnal, sold under sin. [15] For what I am doing, I do not understand. For what I will to do, that I do not practice; but what I hate, that I do. [16] If, then, I do what I will not to do, I agree with the law that *it is* good. [17] But now, *it is* no longer I who do it, but sin that dwells in me. [18] For I know that in me (that is, in my flesh) nothing good dwells; for to will is present with me, but *how* to perform what is good I do not find. [19] For the good that I will *to do*, I do not do; but the evil I will not *to do*, that I practice. [20]

Now if I do what I will not *to do,* it is no longer I who do it, but sin that dwells in me.

²¹ I find then a law, that evil is present with me, the one who wills to do good. ²² For I delight in the law of God according to the inward man. ²³ But I see another law in my members, warring against the law of my mind, and bringing me into captivity to the law of sin which is in my members. ²⁴ O wretched man that I am! Who will deliver me from this body of death? ²⁵ I thank God—through Jesus Christ our Lord!

So then, with the mind I myself serve the law of God, but with the flesh the law of sin.

It is obvious to me that Paul suffered from the same things we suffer from today: his human will, the God-created inward member he warred against every day of his life. The truth is, it will always be inside us. But as Paul said, even if we acknowledge this will of man, this inward member, the law of the mind and the law of the flesh are at war, bringing man into captivity. The human will is not designed to do good, but to follow the law of the flesh, and that is when it is strongest and cannot be defeated. So I am surrendering to it daily according to the desires of the flesh. When it come to the mind, I find that only when it reflects the word of Jesus Christ can it have the power to defeat the human will, as it is written Matthew 4:1–11:

Then Jesus was led up into the wilderness to be tempted by the devil. And when had fasted forty days and forty nights, afterward he was hungry. Now when the tempter came to him, he said, "If you are the son of God, command these stone to become bread." But He answered and said, "It is written, 'Man shall not live by bread alone, but by every word that proceeds from the mouth of God.'" Then the devil took him up into the holy city, set him on a pinnacle of the temple, and said to him, "If you are the son of God, throw yourself down, for it is written: 'He shall give his angels charge over you, in their hands they shall bear you up, lest you dash your foot against a stone.'" Jesus said to him, "It is written again, 'You shall not tempt the Lord your God.'" Again the devil took him up on an exceedingly high mountain, and showed him all the kingdoms of the world and their glory. And he said to him, "All these things will I give you if you will fall down and worship me." Then Jesus said to him, "Away with you Satan, for it is written, 'You shall worship the Lord your God, and him only you shall serve.'" Then the devil left him, and behold, angels came and ministered to him. 4 Then Jesus was led up by the Spirit into the wilderness to be tempted by the devil. ² And when He had fasted forty days and forty nights, afterward He was hungry. ³ Now when the tempter came to Him, he said, "If You are the Son of God, command that these stones become bread."

⁴ But He answered and said, "It is written, 'Man shall not live by bread alone, but by every word that proceeds from the mouth of God.'"[a]

⁵ Then the devil took Him up into the holy city, set Him on the pinnacle of the temple, ⁶ and said to Him, "If You are the Son of God, throw Yourself down. For it is written:

'He shall give His angels charge over you,' and,

'In *their* hands they shall bear you up,

Lest you dash your foot against a stone.'"[b]

⁷ Jesus said to him, "It is written again, 'You shall not tempt the LORD your God.'"[c]

⁸ Again, the devil took Him up on an exceedingly high mountain, and showed Him all the kingdoms of the world and their glory. ⁹ And he said to Him, "All

these things I will give You if You will fall down and worship me."

[10] Then Jesus said to him, "Away with you,[d] Satan! For it is written, 'You shall worship the Lord your God, and Him only you shall serve.'"[e]

[11] Then the devil left Him, and behold, angels came and ministered to Him.

It was the words of Jesus that caused the tempter to leave him alone, and it will be the same in our case: we must first know the word, and then we must apply it when we are at war with our own will. The will of man knows the word of God, just as the devil knew it, even though it was not to his liking or his pleasure, and he had no power over the words of Jesus. The devil left out some very important information when he quoted Psalms 91:11–12: "For he shall give his angels charge over you, to keep you in all your ways. In their hands they shall bear you up, lest you dash your foot against a stone." Even though the devil tempted Jesus, it was Jesus who got the scripture correct—and Satan knew he was doomed because the next verse Jesus quoted confirmed the previous command of God about Jesus defeating Satan. God told the devil to his face that the Son of Man would destroy him by treading on his head with his heel: "And I will put enmity between you and the woman, and between your seed and her seed; he shall bruise his head and he shall bruise his heel" (Gen. 3:15). Given that prognosis, it appears that Satan chose not to quote the scripture that would be used against him, so he casually skipped this verse. But Jesus, being God in the flesh, quoted the scriptures with authority to remind the devil that he was talking to God. In other words, Jesus was saying, "I am your God. Don't tempt me, and don't worship or serve any other god."

The way the will works is like this: it will do whatever it can to have its way, for it already knows who is the authority, and it will submit to the authority of man only when man tells it that he is the authority and that it must obey the will of his mind, which is inspired by his heart. The will cannot yield to the mind alone, for if the mind is not controlled by the spirit of God, the will of man will have control over both the mind and the man. We can also see this result when people try to have control over the spirit without the spirit of God being present in them. As it was with the seven sons of Sceva in Acts 19:14, when the will dominates the man, it soon will take the man into a direction that's different than he ever intended. The true picture is very clear here: man is forever evil, or at least his will is, and no matter how he tries to control himself, there is always a human will in his constitution. As Paul declares in Romans 7:18, "I know that good itself does not dwell in me, that is, in my sinful nature." The "me" Paul is talking about is the "me" that he has no control over—but he has no intention of surrendering to it, either. The catch here is that he admits he has a sinful nature—something everyone must first realize in order to survive. When man realizes this, it usually gives way to the truth. And as Paul so plainly puts it, it is not the God in me that sins, it is the man in me. Paul properly describes it as his "sinful nature"

I have found on my Christian journey that most self-professed "Christians" will not allow themselves to be seen as sinners, even though their sinful nature is greater than their godly behavior. It is a simple case of "I refuse to see myself as I am; therefore, I can be whatever I want to be, even though I can often be a liar. Just let me be—the way of life affords us this privilege." But Paul counters that line of thought in Romans 7:21–22, when he writes, "So I find this law at work: although I want to do good, evil is right there with me, for in my inner being I delight in God's law; but I see another law working in me, waging war against the law of my mind and making me a prisoner of the law of sin at work within me."

The will of man leads the charge against good, and everything works in its favor. If not put in check, it will, as evil does, destroy whatever it touches—even the mind—for it seems that when we want to do good, evil wants us to do bad. But in my soul I have the law of God, the law of love and grace and mercy, but in my mind I have the law of sin, which feeds me thoughts of dissention, confusion, and depression, and which at some point will become deceit. I must remind myself constantly that the light of God is in me, and that we are all blessed with the love of God despite the choices we make.

The will of man is so powerful that it causes a war that can be fought only from one side. The will seeks to win against its creator—not by fighting the creator, but by destroying its host. For the human will knows that the Father is in the man, and the man's mind is all it can control, as the only thing the mind can do is obey or disobey. The will of God's law, on the other hand, cannot be defeated. Even if the man makes his bed in hell, the love of God will be with him. As it was written in Psalms, and as David declared, God does not become infested with the sins of a man's mind, but the mind can become sinful at its core, and every thought can be the basis of sin. Even when the way a man thinks is the opposite of what God wants from him, he still has the great love of God sitting across the room in the hall of his mind. God is just waiting for man to cry out for help arresting this will and taking back control of his thoughts. For if we try to control the mind ourselves, through sinful thoughts, we often become its victims, instead; if we play with fire, we will get burned, for the very nature of sin is to kill, steal, and destroy. But the nature of God is life, and to give life to those who will receive it.

Most of us today have already reached a point of no return—we love the flesh, and there is no going back. So if we want to love the things of God, we must realize that the love of the flesh is right there with us, too, because the first law of nature is self-preservation. Consider the fact that vanity is a trillion-dollar industry: we try everything we can to preserve this flesh. It does not matter who or what we are, we want this flesh to live, and we do everything to keep it from deteriorating. What is alarming is the things we do to beautify the flesh: we make it up, sew it up, tuck it up, prop it up, and touch it up. And as we have seen in current events, people with money even try recreating the flesh: we are growing body parts and attaching them to decaying humans, attaching old cloth to new skins. If we only understood that the old will never be new and the new will always became old, we could simply leave things alone and let God's design for us become as he wants it to be—perfect. I truly believe that anything God creates is and forever will be perfect, because God himself is perfect. Therefore the will of man is perfectly designed to bring God glory and do whatever God wants. The plan of God is made manifest by the will of God, and I have accepted this will as supreme. It has so many sub-wills in it, including the will of man, which is justified by God's will. God the father said he made evil, for it owns day, and the will of man is evil. And in Romans 7:24, Paul refers to the will as "death": "Oh wretch that I am! Who will deliver me from this body of death?"

In my opinion, there is no good in man, yet we continue to look for it. That's why man is considered foolish: he believes he is the author of it every good work he does. But I say to the world that if any good comes from man, it will not come from his will but from God's, for it is God who is good, and anything that is good comes from God. For the rest of human existence, man will have to give way to a greater will than his own. Even when we are perfected, when God has recreated us to be just like him, we will only be copies of the original; we cannot *be* the original at any point of our transformation. God gave every one of his creations its identity, and each creation will forever be identified that way, as a secondary life force. The will of man must always be secondary to the will of God, simply because the will of God gave birth to it, and the order of origination cannot be changed. So even when we feel that we no longer have control over our will, all we need to do is turn to the greater will, which will give us the power to control a will gone wild.

God's will is so powerful over all other wills that if you allow it to replace your human will, it can achieve every good work you need it to do. For instance, the greatest war I fought within my body was the war against my addiction to cigarettes. I tried every way I could to stop smoking, and I just could not "out-will" the addiction. But the very moment I realized that the will of God was stronger than the will of nicotine, I simply put the cigarettes down and never smoked them or even craved them again. The will of God overpowered the will of man. Once God's will comes into its rightful place in your mind, it will never allow your human will to have the final say-so in your life. It will speak for you and, in some cases, totally remove the memory of whatever problem you had.

If man wants to gain positive ground, he must first put on positive shoes to gain traction so he won't slip backwards into past sins or involve himself in new ones. I have learned that truth and honesty can supplant lies and deception in all cases, and that the real reason man lies is not because something or someone makes him do it, but usually because he has sinful desires in his heart. The only way to stop him from lying and deception is to remove the desires or to control the thoughts in his mind that created them. When we give the truth to a man, it does not change the man; it simply gives the man an opportunity to remove the lies and replace them with the truth. We must believe that we can do this and hold on to this hope.

Could it be that the will of man is actually his enemy, not given to man to assist him in his daily life? The only explanation that comes to mind is that we fight from within in order to win within, and therefore we need a reason and a foe to fight. I have concluded that the foe and the reason are one and the same. They are embodied in the will of man, which is inside every man and which is his greatest enemy, commanding him and making suggestions to him on a daily basis. The truth about this will is that it was created to resist God's will, which also is in the heart of a man. The human will has a profound effect upon man's mind, body, and soul, but the will of God has an even greater effect on them—so much so that the man has the great blessing of choice in everything he attempts to do. Even in his choice of thoughts, God's will is present along with man's, although the function of man's will is obvious: it always remains the same, insisting on its own way or no way at all. It simply refuses to compromise. So the man must choose which way he will go. In my own life, I once decided what to do based on the knowledge that was available to me, but now that I am aware of both the persuasive power of human will and the presence of God's will, the choices I make are totally different than the ones I would have made in my youth. Just because a thought comes to mind does not mean that I have to follow it through with it; I have a choice, and the choice should always reflect what is good for me and everyone else involved. It should not be a response to the human will in me. If I obey the law of God's will, I will always win, and everyone involved will win, too.

The will of man has many faces, characteristics, and traits. Sometimes it appears to be good and clean, but the truth is, it is never good and it cannot be clean, because it was made to be just the opposite, and therein lies its purpose. It is a thief and a robber, and it can even become a killer or a murderer. The will of man eagerly pursues sin, as it has from the beginning, when man was newly created and considered to be in the best state he has ever been in. Genesis 2:7 describes that creation: "God formed man of the dust of the ground, and breathed into his nostrils the breath of life, and man became a living being." I can now say with confidence that the breath of life came from God, and God alone, and that the God who gave that breath was and will forever be good. So man was not created bad; he was created good. And everything he does, good or bad, is because of his own will.

Genesis 1:24–31 lays out God's design for the perfect world that man would inhabit:

Then God said, "Let the earth bring forth living creatures according to its own kinds: cattle and creeping things and beasts of the earth, each according to its own kinds," and it was so. And God made the beast of the earth according to its kind, cattle according to its kind and everything that creeps on the earth according to its kind, and God saw that it was good. Then God said, let us make man in our own image, according our own likeness; let them have dominion over the fish of the sea, over the birds of the air, and over the cattle, over all the earth and over every creeping thing that creeps on the earth. So God created man in his own image; in the image of God he created him; male and female he created them. Then God blessed them and God said to them, "Be fruitful and multiply; fill the earth and subdue it; have dominion over the fish of the sea, over the birds of the air, and everything that moves on the earth." And God said, "I give you every herb that yields seeds that on the face of the earth, every tree whose fruit yields seed, to you it shall be for food. Also every beast of the earth, every bird of the air, everything that creeps on the earth, in which there is life, I have given every green herb for food; and it was so. Then God saw everything that he had made, and indeed it was very good. So the evening and the morning were the sixth day. [24] Then God said, "Let the earth bring forth the living creature according to its kind: cattle and creeping thing and beast of the earth, *each* according to its kind"; and it was so. [25] And God made the beast of the earth according to its kind, cattle according to its kind, and everything that creeps on the earth according to its kind. And God saw that *it was* good.

[26] Then God said, "Let Us make man in Our image, according to Our likeness; let them have dominion over the fish of the sea, over the birds of the air, and over the cattle, over all[a] the earth and over every

creeping thing that creeps on the earth." [27] So God created man in His *own* image; in the image of God He created him; male and female He created them. [28] Then God blessed them, and God said to them, "Be fruitful and multiply; fill the earth and subdue it; have dominion over the fish of the sea, over the birds of the air, and over every living thing that moves on the earth."

[29] And God said, "See, I have given you every herb *that* yields seed which *is* on the face of all the earth, and every tree whose fruit yields seed; to you it shall be for food. [30] Also, to every beast of the earth, to every bird of the air, and to everything that creeps on the earth, in which *there is* life, *I have given* every green herb for food"; and it was so. [31] Then God saw everything that He had made, and indeed *it was* very good. So the evening and the morning were the sixth day.

Here the word of God has correctly established man and his condition to the point that we can safely say that he was created good, as was everything else that God made. Therefore I make my stand that it was man, not God, who actually caused man to have the problem of a bad will. When God said he made man in his own image, he never said that he gave man his human will. I also believe that in the transferring of life's breath from God to man, there were no will involved in that process. God simply gave man the best he had, and that's why even the angels questioned God about the blessings he bestowed on man, made in God's very image. They wanted to know what was special about man, that God would be so mindful of him. Could it be that the blood of man is envied by the angels? Or could it be that the man has free will, which he can choose to follow (or not), and yet he is considered by God as his equal? Or could it be that the angels have already been judged, while man is graced to choose what god he will serve and to worship whom he will, and God still loves him? As it is stated in John 3:16, "For God so loved the world he gave his only begotten son, that whoever believes in him should not perish but have everlasting life." That's how much God loved this man, that he created him even in the presence of jealous angels.

I often wonder how the birds of the air really felt when this man arrived and was given dominion over them. It is obvious that they must have had an advantage over the earthbound creatures, and that it must have been difficult for them to look down on man yet have to look up to him, too. That will forever be their plight: man will always be God's preferred creation, and even the lilies of the field will always be secondary to man, for it was God himself who said that none of them was as beautiful as man. God simply loved man and everything about him, so much so that he gave him his own free will. I believe the sons of man were also jealous of him, along with Satan. Job 1:6 describes the scene when they came before God: "Now there was a day when the sons of God came to present themselves before the lord, and Satan also came among them." God knew that Job was his faithful servant, and that no matter what test Satan put to him, he would survive. The way Job had lived his life, he would always come to a place of repentance, because he knew that God loved him and would never leave him or forsake him.

Here is what I believe God said: "I love man enough for him to have his own will, if and when he finds it, for to give man a will is to give him the opportunity to choose for himself, to have or not to have." It was as simple as that. Man was created to love and relate to his creator. It was never God's design for man to become a rebellious creature. As I have stated, God originally created man in his own image, and the reflection was totally good and acceptable to God himself, this supreme creation having been approved by God the Father, Son, and Holy Ghost. When man entered the scene, he was a good and perfect creation of God. As we now know, the problem came later, when man discovered his free will. That is where we began to fail as a creation.

To this day we have not altogether learned why we even need a will. Once we were enlightened and it was revealed to us that we had a will, we instantly put it to the test—and as soon as we did, man's will became his downfall. Here is how it happened: When man was alone with God, he didn't have to choose between right and wrong, because everything he did was with God, and everything was perfect with God, including man, until man was given woman. Woman was given the freedom to choose her relationships, whether it was with the flowers or the animals, and she could and did choose to be with something other than her husband, and that appears to be the first clue to why they failed. When we as human beings choose something other than what God has chosen for us for fellowship, we soon develop problems from those relationships. Man was not chosen for anything but to relate to God, serve God's purpose, and give God glory. Because man was the only creature designed in God's image, it is only logical that God's enemy would to try and force man to turn on God or break his commandments. We see that enemy at work in Genesis 3:1–13:

> Now the serpent of God was more cunning than any beast of the field which God had made. And he said to the woman, "Has God indeed said, 'You shall not eat of every tree of the garden?'" And the woman said to the serpent, "We may eat the fruit of the trees of the garden: but the fruit of the tree which is in the midst of the garden, God has said, 'You shall not eat it, nor shall you touch it, lest you die.'" Then the serpent said to the woman, "You shall not surely die, for God knows that on the day you eat of it your eyes will be opened, and you will be like God, knowing good and evil." So when the woman saw the tree was good for food, that it was pleasant to the eyes, and a tree desirable to make one wise, she took of its fruit and ate, she also gave to her husband with her, and he ate. Then the eyes of both of them were opened, and they knew they were naked; and they sewed fig leaves together to make them coverings. And they heard the sound of the lord walking the garden in the cool of the day, and Adam hid themselves from the presence of the lord God among the trees of the garden. Then the lord called Adam and said to him, "Where are you." So he said, "I heard your voice in the garden, and I

was afraid because I was naked; and I hid myself." And he said, "Who told you that you were naked? Have you eaten from the tree which I commanded you not to eat?" Then the man said, "The woman whom you gave to be with me, she gave of the tree, and I ate." And the lord said to the woman, "What is this you have done?" The woman said, "The serpent deceived me, and I ate."

As we can see, the man's will was used for a different reason than it had originally been intended by God; it coerced him into doing something different than what he was accustomed to doing. When he was with God he did not have to choose what to do—he just did what he wanted to do, and it was good. But when the woman entered the picture, the man had choices that had never even entered his mind. I believe that the Lord's instruction to Adam was not intended to handicap him, but to empower him. That was a good plan until Adam received a different will—and that must have come along with the new companion. For it was her suggestion to eat the fruit and touch the tree; up until then, Adam did everything according the Lord God's instructions. And I believe it would have remained that way for all eternity until Adam received the will to choose right and wrong, and that began with his eating of the forbidden fruit and, even earlier, his companionship with Eve. When he was no longer equal with this woman but her head, he instantly gained his own will. It was for Adam to be the lord to his wife, as God was the lord to him, so he now allowed his mind to entertain thoughts that would lead him to eat the fruit and touch the tree forbidden to him. That's when he realized he had a will to choose, because he remembered what the Lord God told him not to do—and he did it anyway. So before eating of the tree, he chose evil, for he was commanded by God not to eat or touch, and he did what he wanted to do. That's when man's will was established, that's when he went astray, and that's when God created a plan to recapture man's soul, eternally pursuing him to bring him back into fellowship with God.

This situation could have been—and should have been—avoided. I don't believe God needed man to fall in order to have a good relationship him, because it was a good relationship from the beginning. Unfortunately, the will of man is now established, cursing him forever. It was God who put the curse on man, and the only way man can remove the curse is to use the same will he used to disobey God. He can use this same will to obey God, because God inserted a provision that gives man a perfect way to be redeemed, and that is to receive the gift of salvation through the shed blood of Jesus Christ. No other way will suffice, because this provision is a gift for the fallen man, not a reward. Man needs only to repent for his sins and let the Lord hear it from his heart, as Paul tells us in Romans 10:9–10: "That if you confess with your mouth the Lord Jesus and believe in your heart that God has raised him from the dead, you will be saved, for it is the heart that one believes unto righteousness, and with the mouth confession is made unto salvation."

I often pray that out of the ashes of common thought will arise the real truth: that man cannot control his own will if it is not subject to the will of God. Although it is not man's intention, he must submit to the God that made him, because God made him with a will and the first man used his will to disobey the God he knew and loved. This is not to say that there was no temptation at hand—the very tempter that caused Eve to talk about the tree that God forbade them to touch. This story is often told as man's betrayal of God, but in fact it was also an angel's betrayal of God. This must have been very painful for the Creator, to find that his creatures were busy betraying him together. It was as if he had a full rebellion on his hands, a mutiny on the ship we call the Garden of Eden. I often ask myself, *If man was not aware of his betrayal, what was he thinking when he agreed with his wife to touch and eat of the tree? We* are all given the great opportunity to follow the precise instruction of God and obey his perfect will for our life, and I believe that when we obey God and follow the roadmap that he provides, we will forever be blessed and eventually have total control over our own will.

We tend to do just one of two things all the time: we do right, or we do wrong. And it does not matter if we follow God's word or our human will—the only way for man to find peace is for him to accept the God who found him. We are all saved from the beginning, and if man accepts his destiny, he will not have a problem accepting his beginning and the means of his creation. God made man with woman inside him, and then woman was separated from him and became his wife. They both were loved by God, and he walked and talked with them daily. When man sinned, he knew he had done wrong, and so when God attempted to take his daily walk with the man and his wife, something appeared to be different. God was there in the garden, and all his hosts were there, but where were the man and his wife? I can see the fig tree, speaking in its own language, telling God to look at its branches and see the place where the leaves were removed, for it must have been very painful for the tree to have its leaves snatched away like that. Not only was Adam guilty of violating the fig tree, but he also hid behind other trees which, like the fig tree, simply revealed his position. He could not hide from God.

As this first man, Adam, repeated his mistake that we now call "sin," it is necessary for us to see the truth about his creation and the reason for it. We have to ask ourselves, *What was God thinking when he made man this way? What was he after when gave man free will? Why did man need a will?* I often hear people say in explaining their behavior, "The devil made me do it," or some variation on that theme. With a consistence beyond comprehension, they blame someone other than themselves. Well, that may not be so far-fetched after all. There might be a third party involved or a hidden enemy who wields a powerful influence on its host. I have come to believe that that hidden enemy is man's own will, which is alive and substantive, and which can (and usually does) take control over man's mind—and "as a man thinks, so is he." Once the mind conceives of the thought, inspired by the will, it will always lead him into sin, and once sin is conceived, it leads to death. So this freedom of choice has become the very tool the enemy of God needs to get man to sin against God.

We are often driven by a thought that we never examine, but the origination of a thought is just as important as the thought itself. When we give way to the thought, we give way to its source, and as we come to find out, sometimes we realize too late that the thought came from an enemy we didn't even know existed: this thing called the will of man. It will cause you to forget the substance of the very thought it gives you, and before you know it, you are destroyed by it. When the church that we call a place of worship become a place of torment or bondage, you will not even know that you are trapped until you find yourself in deep trouble.

Why we continue to do things that are not good for us is not always clear, for it seems we should have known better. But it never fails—we didn't see it coming, or we just didn't want to see anything except what we believed we saw. As wrong as it is, we continue to go along just to get along, not even realizing that the only reason we are where are is because we were either enticed or fooled into believing a lie. That was exactly the case with Eve, the first woman, who gave way to her own curiosity and allowed her will to put her in a place where the devil could lie to her. She believed him long enough to be enticed into sin. As we often do, she followed the advice of her own will, the very thing that drew her there to begin with. It is very clear to me that God punished the right ones for the right sin: Eve was punished for her sin, Adam was punished for his sin, and Satan was punished for his. It was simply their own wills that led them to sin, giving them the freedom they needed to choose. And when man chooses without God's influence, he always chooses wrong.

At the end of the day, man needs God's will to control his own. For as we've witnessed with Adam and Eve, the freedom to choose does not mean you will choose the right thing. It simply means you will have the freedom to do right or wrong. God never intended for man to fail; he never gave man a flawed nature. God gave man a good heart and a strong mind, a solid foundation upon which to establish himself and enjoy the garden he and Eve shared. Man had free will to do what he wanted, and once he used it to break God's covenants or do what God said not to do, it became infected with sin. When sin entered into the world, everything became contaminated, and it will take God himself to cleanse it and make it good again. Man cannot remove sin from his will or his mind or his soul; only God can do that. And that is what God decided to do—restore his creation through the only appropriate sacrifice. So he made a new Adam, the Christ, the Son of God, the son of man, in order to redeem the mess that man made. God alone had to do it, for there was no one else worthy of the challenge. God made man, and man made a mess. Man had nothing to give, and God gave his best. According to John 3:16, "For God so loved the world that he gave his only begotten son, that whosoever would believe in him shall not perish but have everlasting life."

God gave man the power over his will when he gave man his own son as a sacrifice for man's sins. If man would accept his son, he would have power over the will that destroyed the first man. We are very much in need of this power today. You see, when we accept this gift of life, which is Jesus Christ, the next-greatest miracle happens in our life: the Holy Spirit comes into it and weaves itself into the very fibers of our physical and spiritual DNA. We become new creatures, and immediately the change takes place, just as God promised. The Spirit comes upon us, and once this happens, there is no turning back.

Consider the story of the woman at the well (John 4:7–26). When she met Jesus, he became the seventh man in her life, at the seventh hour, at the seventh well. She spoke with him and questioned him, and then she accepted him—and instantly her life was changed forever. This woman's human will led her to serve man in the capacity of wife or girlfriend, but when she met Jesus, she accepted his offer of water that would forever satisfy her thirst. She received by faith the water of eternal life, and in this way she accepted the will of God. She dropped her old water jars and her old lifestyle and ran to town to tell the people about a man who seemed to know everything she ever did. Then she asked them a question that she already knew the answer to: Could this be the messiah? It is obvious that this woman no longer gave her will total control over her mind, body and soul; she now was under the divine will of Jesus Christ.

We can see this very point being made in the story of another man, Zacchaeus, who had the unsavory job of taking money from people. We read in Luke 19:1–10 that Jesus came into Jericho and saw a man who was very small in stature but very large in wealth. He was a chief tax collector; he had taken people's money and even cheated them. It was his will, not God's, that he did these things, but for some reason the Lord had mercy on him, calling to him and offering to stay with him in his own house, to the disgust of the other Jews. As soon as he came to Jesus, Zacchaeus began to repent and confess to the Lord. And what is more important is that he publicly said he would give half of what he had to the poor and pay back four times the amount of money he'd gotten from cheating people. So much of his life was driven by greed—his will was to steal and cheat—that nothing could have stopped him or changed his ways except Jesus. Now Zacchaeus, the chief tax collector, had the divine will of God, and his behavior reflected the change in his heart. God's will was now in his heart, and it would forever be present in him, no matter what temptations he faced.

That brings me to my conclusion—the point of change in my own life that left me in the best possible situation. I am not ashamed of my past or the will that once ruled my every decision. It started a long time ago. From my earliest memory it was very clear to me that I had a will of my own. It was in 1965, and I was five years old. As a matter of fact, it was summer, and I had the joy of living in the Deep South, where folks just lived as best they could. We lived in the housing projects, which to me was simply "home," and nothing more. My mother was what you would call a true homemaker—a provider and wife, a friend and a keeper for her sister's children. She also was a maid for several white families—and God only knows what else she did. I think that's why I felt the need to stay close by my mother and enjoy her presence, because she simply had too much to do. I'll always believe that she worked herself to death.

Anyway, I was in the backyard, and as I remember it, I was drawn to the edge of the woods at the rear of the yard, and it was there that I first met the Lord. Every day I went out to that spot, and as I walked into the woods I would always hear the same voice saying the same thing: *You will preach my Gospel.* Not knowing what the Gospel was or who was talking to me, I would go inside immediately and tell my mother. This happened day after day, and somewhere in the middle of the summer, my mother finally said, "Stay out of them woods!" But the following day I returned. I was hard-headed, and it's evidence of my strong will that I went back into those woods over and over again until the end of that summer. My will was to do what I wanted to do, despite my mother's instruction. The last time I heard the man in the woods, I saw him, too. That's when I finally responded to the voice and noticed his image. He had a very pleasant appearance and was peaceful-sounding. But even as a five-year-old boy, I began arguing with him. I told him that I would not preach unless he would give me the power to stop my father from beating on my mother, that I would not preach unless he cured my aunt's cancer and made the Holy Ghost save everyone in the world. That was the last visit I had with him, and my last memory of that summer.

Even at age five, I had a will to say no to God, and I didn't even understand the consequences of my action. But that would begin a life of total hell for me—a life that continued until I accepted the will of God.

It has been said that when a bad man meets a good God, the will of that bad man surrenders to the good God, and the will of that man become secondary to the will of God. I know this to be true, and I have written this book so that others may know that the will of man is a substantive being that can cause you to go against the very God that created you and gave you that will. As for me, it is now my choice to serve the Lord, preach his Gospel, and forever obey him. I will never again refuse him, no matter what he asks of me. I will go and do anything God requests of me. I am proud to be a preacher and a prophet for my Lord and your God—*Jesus Christ, the savior of the world.*

A warning to all mankind: it is impossible for God to lie, and he said, "for whatever a man sows, that shall he also reap." The truth is, we must not allow our will to control us and cause us to sin against God and our flesh. As it stands, the only thing that can stop this will from destroying us is the will of God, which will lead us and guide us to a more blessed life. In the heart of man is a will that he received as a gift from his first earthly father, Adam, who followed that will and was therefore separated from God.

It is obvious to me that what is said in Matthew 4:4 is true, that a man cannot live by bread alone. In this case, the bread of man is his own will. Instead, man must live on the bread of God—God's will and his word. Still, we were born with this human will, a gift with which we can freely choose whatever we want. Often it becomes a yoke around our neck, a problem that cannot be easily removed or handled. So the greatest accomplishment we could ever have is to accept the will of God and deny this thing that we call free will. Once we accept God's will, our lives will take a very different path. The problem we all have is that we trust our intuition. We believe that if our mind tells us our decision is okay, there's nothing wrong with it. But the truth is, once we go against God's will, we cannot adjust the outcome.

So when we are faced with such a decision, we should first reconsider the subject or the thought, examining it thoroughly and in depth. In this way, we can discover other options that we might have missed had we acted on the first impulse that came to mind. Our human will is no more than our imagination with intelligence; whatever it comes up with, it believes it can do, despite the outcome. Much like a parasitic organism, its sole purpose is to feed on its host and reproduce to the detriment of that host. Once a man's will has its way, it will destroy its own host. It's like having a passenger riding with a drunk man, coaching him along until the man is no longer driving the car but just holding the steering wheel—until the man looks over and notices that the passenger is no longer in the car, and he dies alone in a terrible crash. At that point it's too late to regain control of your life, and unfortunately for many of us, that's the very moment we begin to realize the seriousness of our situation.

We will ourselves into this type of mess, and sometimes we have to will ourselves out of it. The only way to do that is to pay close attention to the things that got us into the mess in the first place. You must carefully monitor your human will every day of your life, so that you'll know when you're developing a habit that does not benefit you, that can destroy relationships and maybe even cause you to lose your very life. Keep in mind that a bad idea will always appear at first as a good idea, a better way to do things. The will of man is never a silent partner; it is always very vocal, and it wants to control you and lead you through life. Don't surrender to it, for it is the will that should surrender to you.

I am sure of one fact about the will of man: it is self-destructible, because it is contaminated by evil. I often wonder why man never realized that his true enemy lay within, as Eve lay within the created man Adam. I believe that when she accepted Satan's challenge, she joined Satan as the Adam's enemy.

The man who respects his own limitations will not overrun his destination. I am forever seeking to understand the human will inside me. It appears to work in unison with the clock of the flesh, at times speeding up the body's clock so that death comes prematurely. God's will is for man to live and not die, but man's will is to return to his original state, to rejoin the dust of the earth. I often wonder why man behaves in such a self-destructive way, because I've heard that the first law of nature is self-preservation, and if that's true, then the last law of nature would have to be self-destruction, man's will.

It is very clear to me that if I will something, it will be, and if I don't will something, it will not be, or I will never get the pleasure of possessing that thing. Therefore the will of man must control our thoughts, and the only way to prevent it from leading us somewhere we do not wish to be is to say no to the will and yes to what is good and righteous—the will of God, which is in our spirit. If we do what we don't want to do, we are only doing what the will of man wants us to do. So we must not give in to a will that we know will cause problems. The only way to manage it is to take control of it as you must also control your flesh, and not be led by the will of man, which is opposed to the will of God. God's will is for you to do what you know to be good and righteous.

I wish to congratulate every one of you for reading this book and accepting the simple fact that we all were given a will, the innate force that God gave man to help him return to his original physical state: from dust he came, and to dust he will return. The difference between man's will and his spirit is that the will is earthbound and the spirit is heaven-bound. A mind controlled by the will is allowed to dominate the man. If the human will wins, the mind has already lost the battle of preserving the flesh. And if the flesh is lost, then the soul and spirit have no body in which to live.

We are often pulled between doing the right thing and doing the wrong thing, and yet we never ask ourselves why. What if there are two wills—the will of God and the will of man—battling within our mind? We should question ourselves every time we have a decision before us that might affect our present and future. Sometime we desire things without knowing why, so I've developed a simple test to determine whether or not the desire I have is good or bad: if what I desire benefits me and others, then it is my spirit that controls the desire and it is good. But if the desire might harm me or others, it is my flesh that controls the desire, and it is bad. For I have learned that this flesh of mine cannot desire any good thing; it always leads me into a deficit. A man who understands that good is the better way is a man who has power over his own will, for he will choose to do good rather than evil.

The purpose of man's will is to assist him—that's not in question—but what is in question is why God created that will. I do believe that if left to his own devices, man would destroy himself, anyway. He would return to his original condition: helpless, worthless, and without purpose. And if he does not accept God's will for his life, he will return to the dust completely, for even if he does accept God's will for his life, he will still lose his flesh to the earth from which it came, but the soul will return to God. So the man who follows his own will has but one destination: dust and destruction. We cannot deny the facts. The will of man is the culprit for our sins, and its benefactor is the enemy of God.

Therefore it is man's sole responsibility to follow the will of God and live within the boundaries of God's expectations for his life—simply put, to love God and to love his own neighbors as he loves himself. Amen.

CPSIA information can be obtained at www.ICGtesting.com
Printed in the USA
LVOW042229140912

298794LV00004B/292/P